What do they call pastors in Germany? German Shepherds

What kind of cell phone did Delilah use?...

Samson

How long did Cain hate his brother? ...

As long as he was Abel to.

Why couldn't Jonah trust the ocean?... He just knew there was something fishy about it.

How do we know Peter was a rich fisherman?... By his net income.

Why didn't Noah ever go fishing?... He only had two worms.

Who was the smartest man in the Bible? ... Abraham. He knew a Lot.

What kind of person was Boaz before he got married? ... Ruthless!

Who was the greatest comedian in the Bible? ... Samson. He brought the house down.

Which servant of God was the worst lawbreaker in the Bible? ... Moses. He broke all 10 commandments at once.

"There will be a meeting of the Church Board immediately after the service," announced the pastor.

After the close of the service, the Church Board gathered at the back of the sanctuary for the announced meeting. But there was a stranger in their midst — a visitor who had never attended their church before.

"My friend," said the pastor, "Didn't you understand that this is a meeting of the Board?"

"Yes," said the visitor, "and after today's sermon, I suppose I'm just about as bored as anyone else who came to this meeting."

At what time of day was Adam created?... A little before Eve.

Which Bible character had no parents?... Joshua, son of Nun.

Early one morning the husband and wife were arguing over who should get out of the warm bed to make the coffee. Finally, the wife folded her arms and said decidedly, "You have to make the coffee. It's in the Bible!"

The husband was shocked. "Is not! Show me!"

Pulling out her Bible, the wife opened it to one of the New Testament books and declared, "It says right here — HEBREWS!"

What animal could Noah not trust?... Cheetah

Who was the straightest man in the Bible?...

Joseph: Pharao made him a ruler

During a Sunday school lesson, a child learned about how God created human beings. The child became especially focused when the teacher explained how Eve was created from Adam's ribs. Later in the week, the boy's mother saw him lying down on the floor, so she asked him what was wrong. His reply was priceless: "Mom, I have a pain in my side—I think I'm getting a wife."

What did Jonah's family say when he told them about what happened before reaching Nineveh?

"Hmm, sounds fishy."

What was Moses' wife, Zipphora, known as when she'd throw dinner parties? "The hostess with the Moses."

A little girl finally got to attend a wedding for the first time. While in the church, the girl asked her mother: "Why is the bride dressed in white?" The mother replied to the girl: "because white is the color of happiness and it's the happiest day of her life today."

After a little bit, the girl looks up at her mother and says: "But, then why is the groom wearing black?"

What did the classmate say when asked why they kept walking next to the same person at school? "I was told I'm supposed to walk by Faith!"

Which Bible character was super-fit? Absalom.

A Kindergarten teacher was observing her classroom as the children drew pictures. The teacher would occasionally walk around and see each child's artwork. As she approached one little girl who was working especially hard, she asked what the drawing was.

The little girl told her: "I'm drawing God!"

"But sweety," the teacher replied, "no one knows what God looks like."

Automatically, the little girl continued drawing and said: "Well, they certainly will in a minute!"

What did Adam say when he was asked his favorite holiday? "It's Christmas, Eve."

What did pirates call Noah's boat? "The arrrrrrk."

After service, a stranger approached the pastor and said, "I'd like you to pray for my hearing."

The pastor placed his hands on the man's ears and said a passionate, earnest prayer.

"How's your hearing now?" the pastor asked.

Looking surprised, the man said, "Well, it's not until tomorrow."

How are toddlers and those who attempted to build a tower to Heaven similar? They all babble.

After the wedding, the little ringbearer asked his father, "How many brides can the groom marry?"

"One," his father said. "Why do you ask?"

"Because the priest said he could marry sixteen," the boy said, puzzled.

"How'd you come up with that?" his father asked.

"Easy," the little boy said. "All you have to do is add it up like the priest said: 4 better, 4 worse, 4 richer, 4 poorer."

Why didn't anyone want to fight Goliath? It seemed like a giant ordeal.

Which king liked to do things on his own?

Solomon

Bent over and obviously in pain, the old man with a cane hobbled laboriously through the sanctuary and into the pastor's office while the choir was practicing.

Ten minutes later he came out, walking upright and moving with grace and speed.

"Good gracious," the choir director exclaimed. "Did the pastor heal you by faith?"

"No," the old man said with a smile. "He just gave me a cane that wasn't six inches too short!"

Why did Adam and Eve do math every day? They were told to be fruitful and multiply.

How do you know that atoms are Catholic? They have mass.

What did Daniel tell his real estate agent? "I'd prefer a house with no den."

Who in the Bible knew the most people? Abraham knew a Lot.

What's a believer's favorite fruit? Spiritual.

How did
Joseph
make his
coffee?
Hebrewed it.

What's loved by Noah and also most meat-eaters? Ham.

How do you know Pharaoh was athletic? He had a court.

When someone needed a boat made, what did the people in town say? "We Noah guy.

What did Zachariah do when he and Elizabeth had disagreements? He gave the silent treatment.

What's a miracle that can be done by a complainer? Turning anything into whine.

After service, a stranger approached the pastor and said, "I'd like you to pray for my hearing."

The pastor placed his hands on the man's ears and said a passionate, earnest prayer.

"How's your hearing now?" the pastor asked.

Looking surprised, the man said, "Well, it's not until tomorrow."

How do pastors like their orange juice? With pulpit.

Who was the fastest runner in the race? Adam. He was first in the human race.

Why didn't they play cards on the Ark? Because Noah was always standing on the deck

Did Eve ever have a date with Adam? Nope — just an apple.

Why did the unemployed man get excited while reading his Bible?

He thought he saw a job.

What's so funny about forbidden fruits? They create many jams.

A little boy in church for the first time watched as the ushers passed around the offering plates. When they came near his pew, the boy said loudly, "Don't pay for me, Daddy, I'm under five."

Who was the first tennis player in the bible?

Joseph because he served in Pharaoh's court

Who is the greatest babysitter mentioned in the Bible? David — he rocked Goliath to a very deep sleep

How do groups of angels greet each other? Halo, halo, halo!

Who was the greatest moneyman in the Bible?

Noah. He was floating his stock while everyone else was in liquidation.

What do we have that Adam never had?
Ancestors.

What did Adam say the day before Christmas? It's Christmas, Eve!

Who do mice pray to? Cheesus.

How do you make Holy Water?

You take some regular water and boil the devil out of it.

Why did Noah have to punish and discipline the chickens on the Ark?

They were using fowl language.

What do donkeys send out near Christmas? Mule-tide greetings.

On the Ark, Noah probably got milk from the cows. What did he get from the ducks? Quackers.

Who was the best female finance lady in the Bible? Pharaoh's daughter. She went down to the bank of the Nile and drew out a little prophet

Which
Bible
Character
is a
locksmith?
Zaccheus.

What's the best way to study the Bible? You Luke into it.

What do you call a sleepwalking nun?

A roamin' Catholic

What do you call a priest who becomes a lawyer? A father-in-law.

Why did the sponge go to church?

It was hole-y.

What did God do to cure Moses' headache? He gave him two tablets.

What did Moses say when he saw people worshipping the golden calf?

Holy cow!

God is talking to one of his angels. He says, "Do you know what I have just done? I have just created 24 hours of alternating light and darkness on Earth. Isn't that good?"

The angel says, "Yes, but what will you do now?"

God says, "I think I'll call it a day."

Where is the best place to get an ice cream cone? Sunday School.

What is a mathematician's favorite book of the Bible? Numbers.

What type of lights did Noah have on the Ark? Floodlights.

Why did Samson try to avoid arguing with Delilah? He didn't want to split hairs.

Which area of
the Promised
Land was
especially
wealthy?
The area around
the Jordan where
the banks kept
overflowing.

Why wouldn't the Pharaoh let the Hebrews go?
He was in 'de Nile.

What is a salesman's favorite Scripture passage? The Great Commission.

What is a missionary's favorite kind of car?

A convertible.

Why is Swiss considered the most religious type of cheese? It's hole-y.

What is a dentist's favorite hymn? Crown him with many crowns.

Why did Moses cross the Red Sea?

To get to the other side.

What did the pastor say to a man with Twitter addiction? - Sorry, I don't follow you.

Fast food is the only food that is permitted to be consumed while fasting because they are fast food.

Why is it that Jesus cannot wear necklaces? Because He is the one who breaks every chain.

So, what did the Jew have to say to the Gentile? "I wish you were Jewish."

What time of day does Adam prefer?

Eve-ning

The pastor and the beer

"If I had all the beer in the world, I'd take it and throw it in the river," a preacher said as he finished a temperance sermon. "And if I had all the drink in the world," he said with humility, "I'd take it and throw it into the river." "And if I had all the whiskey in the world," he finally admitted, "I'd take it and throw it into the river." He slid into a chair. "For our closing song, let us sing Hymn # 365: "Shall We Gather at the River," the song leader said, taking a cautious step forward and smiling.

When Mary found out she was pregnant, what did she say? "Oh, my baby."

What is the court's favourite Bible book?

Judges

A jew asserts, "You won't believe what happened to me, Rabbi! My son has converted to Christianity." The Rabbi responds, "You're not going to believe what happened to *me*! My son also converted to Christianity. Let us pray to God and see what He has to say to us."
"You'll never guess what happened to ME!" God says in response to their prayers.

Both a priest and a taxi driver died and were resurrected. St. Peter was waiting for them at the Pearly Gates. St. Peter motioned to the taxi driver, 'Come with me.' The taxi driver followed St Peter to a mansion as instructed. It had everything imaginable, from a bowling alley to an Olympic-sized pool. 'Oh my word, thank you,' the taxi driver said. St. Peter then led the priest to a run-down shack with a bunk bed and an old television set. 'Wait, I think you're a little confused,' the priest said. 'Shouldn't it be me who gets the mansion?' After all, I was a priest who went to church every day and preached the word of God.' 'That is correct.' 'But during your sermons, people slept,' St Peter countered. Everyone prayed as the taxi driver drove

What did God say after He created Adam? "I can do better than that." And so, He created woman.

If Goliath would come back to life today, would you like to tell him the joke about David and Goliath?
No, he already fell for it once.

Where is a square dance class mentioned in the Bible?

In Jonah 4:11 that says, "There are more than a hundred and twenty thousand people who cannot tell their right hand from their left."

Don't let your worries get the best of you. Remember, Moses started out as a basket case.

Mrs. Smartt was fumbling in her purse for her offering when a large television remote fell out and clattered into the aisle. The curious usher bent over to retrieve it for her and whispered, "Do you always carry your TV remote to church?"

"No," she replied, "but my husband refused to come with me this morning, and I figured this was the most evil thing I could do to him legally."

If you look for it hard enough, it's easy to find Solomon's temple. It's situated near his head.

Moses was known to be a very technologically savvy person. After all, that's why God trusted him with two tablets.

If you don't eat bread while you're in church you'll be toast.

My sister only believes in 20% of the bible. She's an eight-theist.